REQUIEM FOR THE TREE FORT
I SET ON FIRE

Tim Tomlinson

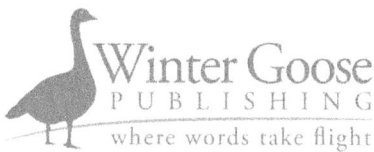

Winter Goose
PUBLISHING
where words take flight

Winter Goose Publishing
45 Lafayette Road #114
North Hampton, NH 03862

www.wintergoosepublishing.com
Contact Information: info@wintergoosepublishing.com

Requiem for the Tree Fort I Set on Fire

COPYRIGHT © 2016 by Tim Tomlinson

First Edition, August 2016

Cover Design by Winter Goose Publishing
Photograph by Tim Tomlinson
Baclayon Church, Bohol, Philippines
Typeset by Odyssey Books

ISBN: 978-1-941058-52-7

Published in the United States of America

TABLE OF CONTENTS

For Charlie Conran, piano player

"If I had a nickel I'd find a game.
If I won a dollar I'd make it rain.
If it rained an ocean I'd drink it dry,
and lay me down dissatisfied."

—Townes Van Zandt, "Rex's Blues"

I

"No one is interested in your precious memories,"
explains the author of best-selling memoirs.

AT NIGHT, AFTER THE SCREAMS

wake us

we hear him walk
to the kitchen,

hear

his callused feet scuff
the hardwood floor, hear

him mutter curses
at the carpet,
its edge

perpetually curled, hear him
go

silent

on the linoleum
of the kitchen
floor.

So much is hidden

by our mother,

in closets

behind cans and boxes.

So much

that he loves—

Mallomars, Mr. Chips,
Hostess Twinkies.

We hear him
rummaging,

rummaging,

the cans clinking,
the boxes tearing open,
and his hands,

his thick
callused hands
ripping

through wax paper
and plastic packaging.

Hear
the refrigerator suck
open,

sense
its light through the cracks

of our bedroom doors.

When he stands
in that cold light,
when he upends the milk carton,
when he douses
the fire

in his throat,
does he wonder, as we
do,

what made him scream,
again,
this time,

his mother's name?

THE JEHOVAH'S WITNESS

The Jehovah's Witness sat
at the dining table drinking Sanka
whitened with Coffee Mate and nibbling

Arrowroot Tea Biscuits. Her tapered skirt
pressed her knees together, her sweater
separated her ice cream cone breasts.

She talked about heaven in the way
I imagined it, dull as a Sunday
suit, but Dad, an avid church-avoider,

leaned forward in his sleeveless t,
his elbows on the table, the veins
in his forearms trailing into the vines

of his tattoos—"Mama" on one arm,
the USMC coat of arms
on the other. His bodybuilding

trophies glistened in the sunlight on
windowsills. He was eating between meals.
Mom came home with the papers

and the jelly doughnuts and the crumb buns.
She put a pint of cream on the table.
"We're Catholic," she said.

The Jehovah's Witness said, "So was I."
"I know what you were," my mother told her.
The Jehovah's Witness stood. She brushed crumbs

from her lap and sweater. "I'll come back,"
she said, "at a better time." Dad stared
holes into her biscuits.

IF WISHES WERE HORSES

With the horses fed, I'd walk him out
the paddock to where his three-speed Schwinn
leaned on the gate. Good kid, full of questions—
what makes horses run, can they always run
faster than grown-ups, how far do they get
before resting? His bike was a racer,
fire engine-red frame, ram horn handlebars,
stripped for speed, not safety. His feet barely
reached the pedals. He'd pull his cap tight,
then push off down the trail, whooping the way
he thought cowboys whooped, lost in a cloud of dust.
I'd go finish up with the horses—
water in the buckets, fresh hay in the bins.
Silky with the white forelock, Commander
with three white socks. Brett, the chestnut,
was the kid's favorite—he was the fastest.
One day, the kid said, *I'm gonna climb up*
on Brett and ride so far so fast
my father will never hit me again.
Seems like the father hit that good kid
a bunch. Some days I'd find him in the hay shed,
choking back tears. Some days I'd find him
banged up with the kind of bruises you don't
get from mucking stalls. Some days, I wished
I could saddle him up myself, swat that chestnut
on the rump with my hat and say *Ha!*

B.A.R. (BROWNING AUTOMATIC RIFLE)

the day after Christmas
        you lie belly down in two feet of snow

and rest
the snout of your new B.A.R. on its bipod
                                 and take aim

                at

trees, at

        mailboxes, at

squirrels shivering naked on
the top steps of your neighbors' stoops and open

fire at

their indifference

                the block is empty of
children,
        of moving targets

the birds don't even flutter

at the clamor bursting from your new weapon
the smoke

pouring from its barrel

the rocks are buried
                              in snow

____

inside, your brother has an idea

with a ball-peen hammer and flathead screwdriver
he busts open
                              the stock and exposes the guts
              of your new gun, the B.A.R.,
where the oil goes,
the oil

              that greases the gears
and makes the smoke and produces the noise
that's louder and more real
                              and more conclusive
and more terrifying

than all the noises from all the kids' guns
on Robinson Street
all the way to the Wheat Fields
                              beyond North Country Road

when he's finished, the B.A.R. makes no noise

the bolt guide, the cylinder, the sling,
the bent springs, twisted coils, limp trigger

the jagged plastic splinters

                           a pile of garbage

    you stare into

    ———

the day after the day

         after Christmas, in two feet of snow

the silence
the trees
    the birds on bare branches, looking

at you

gunless,

your dumb ice-cold

         fury

EIGHT DAYS A WEEK

I don't know it yet, but it's the last day
I'll ever follow my big brother, Wally,
off Knickerbocker Avenue, up Bleecker
toward our grandma's apartment, the Myrtle
Avenue El rumbling behind us. The small
teeth of a slanted comb poke from Wally's
back pocket, his Cuban heels clack
on the sidewalk, his iridescent slacks
shine like gasoline on a puddle.
He's a ten-year-old Frankie Valli.
I'm eight, and one thing I know: big girls might
not cry, but big brothers do. Wally acts
tough, but at the dentist, I hear him howl
so loud I drop my *Boy's Life*. And when Dad
raises his voice, Wally changes his pants.
He can't hack a little pain, or even
the threat of it. I follow him now through
the hot exhaust blowing out the dry cleaner's
vent, past Pete the Jeweler selling watches
from the trunk of a Buick. Mrs. Gentile
sunk her elbows into the pillow on
her windowsill, her lips smeared with ragu.
Corner of Central, Wally runs the comb
through his wings, shoulders up to the window
where an Annette Funicello lookalike
scoops Italian ice into Dixie cups.
He says a lemon ice for him, and can she
heat up some milk for me. It's time for my

nap, he says, like I'm the kid brother,
a pest, an affliction who cramps his style,
and the girl, this candy store Mouseketeer,
laughs right in my face. All I ever want
is to follow Wally, make him see that
I can hang with the big kids, make him laugh,
even act as tough and dumb as his friends.
I want to shrug off this new hurt, show them
I'm not some crybaby punk, when a sound
I've never heard before fades in from
the radio of a Ford Skyliner idling
at the steps of St. Barbara's. Major chords
chiming behind a voice that shoots
like a drug into the pleasure center
of my brain. Later I'll learn how chords can
have false relations, how their false match is
barely perceived, but the discord they make
creates unbreakable bonds. That's not what
I'm thinking when I hear them. I'm not thinking
at all. I'm feeling, and everything that
once felt important—good grades, fast sneakers,
even Wally's approval—suddenly
they're meaningless. When the Skyliner pulls
away, Wally says, *Was that that Beatles
shit?* But I barely hear him now, and it's
like that for several years, until little
by little, I don't hear him at all.

SATISFACTION

It's 1965, I'm nine, Cousin Danny's fifteen.
He's visiting from San Francisco, where he's a high diver,
swimmer, runner, and climber,

and our backyard on Long Island, he says
with great authority, is so boring. As if
I didn't know that, squirting glue

into ant nests and dropping matches
onto the entrances, the large black ants crinkling
as they rush from their homes

through the burnt grass, fleeing from fire
that's stuck on their backs. Tossing crickets
into webs and watching their crazy panic

while spiders spin them into little bags
of meat. Catching bumblebees in glass jars
and leaving them sweating in the sun,

the bright shine of their yellow fur dulling
in the airless heat. In two years it will be
the Summer of Love, with Danny

at its front lines, bearded, beaded, beautiful,
but today he shows me how to remove the legs
from a Daddy Longlegs. The legs continue

to twitch and reach and jackknife as if
they still had somewhere to go, and within minutes,
red ants locate the spider's legless ovoid body,

which they section and carry off, even
as the spider watches. Does the spider see
its own legs there on the patio, escaping

in different directions? Does it see the boys
who will do anything not to feel remorse about
anything they're doing? Does it see that one day

remorse will come, along with the fire, and the ants?

GULF STREAM
for Mike Tomlinson, sailor

Rough now, my feet off the edge
of the sunfish, rushing farther
from the shore where
my father, a mere speck,
paces back and forth in front
of the lifeguard stand, his arms
waving semaphores I pretend
I can't see, no less understand.
I'm beyond his whistle.
It's the Gulf Stream I head for,
its blue ink and the creatures that break
its rough surface—I know
the Winslow Homer painting.
If art is for anything, it's for
getting us away from anything
that holds us back, anything that keeps
us from entering the deep water.
Anything that keeps us from feeling
the fear that owns us anytime
the great gray shadow prowls
beneath the paltry shadow we throw.
In the rough water where
the current quickens and the sail
pulls at its stays, the fear returns to itself,
unable to keep us from heading out
past our limits, the limits of others,
while we do our work.

THE DAY MY GRANDMOTHER FELL OFF THE PORCH

only part of her got back up, the part
that had to prepare my grandfather's

pasta and lentils with cauliflower
every day at noon while the television

blasted game shows he snored in front of.
The part that didn't want to continue

preparing my grandfather's pasta at noon
remained on the bottom step in a heap

with the jagged stump of her femur poking
through her thigh and the smile on her face,

ignoring the complaints he shouted over
The Newlywed Game. That's how we found her.

MESCALINE

On mescaline we walked close to the dunes
where terns nested. They swung into the sky

and dove like arrows aimed straight at our heads.
I wasn't sure if it was happening,

but it was happening, and I watched you run
to the shoreline, fall knee-deep in the surf,

your arms flailing at residual trails
the terns sliced into the ether.

How odd that must have appeared to people
not on mescaline, but how intriguing

to me. Van Morrison's "intrigue of
nature's beauty" occurred to me, how there's

stillness beneath nature's violence
and from that stillness all things radiate.

But that's not what you were thinking when they
pulled you soaked and shivering from the surf.

Later you explained how that one image—
me watching your terror—is what ended

us. That was the danger with mescaline:
the immutable truths it might reveal.

FIVE EASY PIECES
for Barbara McKenna

The boy leaves a screening of *Five Easy Pieces*
transformed,

he's not sure how,

facing traffic on the shoulder of 25A
with his thumb out at his waist.

His first ride carries him

to the fork into Miller Place.
A girl from Miller Place had hurt him.

So had girls from Mt. Sinai,
Sound Beach, Rocky Point, Port Jefferson.

He walked a long way.

He thought about Jack Nicholson,
how he vanished in Alaska.

REQUIEM FOR THE TREE FORT I SET ON FIRE

and requiem for the tree that held it.
Requiem for the woods surrounding
that tree and tree fort, now burnt to charred
stumps and blackened trunks standing like gnomes
over the smoking bark expiring on
ash heaps of scrub oak and scrap pine, cones and
needles, and dying centipedes curling
arthritically their one hundred brittle
legs two or three final times. Requiem
for the smoke, and the smell of the smoke caught
up in the whirlwind and blown over
the towns of Eastern Long Island.

Requiem for the backyards the fire reached.
Requiem for the split rail fences and
the redwood fences and the red hot chain
link fences, vined with ivy now black and
crisp and vaporous. Requiem for
the scorched lawns, the melted wading pools,
the carbonized toys, the steaming swimming
pools and the diving boards' blistered resins.
Requiem for the back decks surrounding
the homes, the redwood staircases leading
to the patio furniture, the crumpled
picnic tables, the aluminum umbrella
poles with vinyl and polyester welded
to their sides. Requiem for the shingles
the fingers of fire climbed. Requiem for

the windowsills. Requiem for the windows—
the ones that burst in the fire, and the ones
the fire crept under, or through, or around.
And requiem for the curtains, requiem
for the blinds. Requiem for the bedrooms
and the beds, the bassinets, and the cribs.
Requiem, requiem, requiem.

Requiem for the upstairs, requiem
for the down, requiem for the basements
and the attics. Requiem for the pool
tables and ping pong tables and punching
bags, requiem for the stacks of *LIFE*
magazine and *National Geographic*,
and requiem for wedding
dresses in boxes, the wedding pictures
blistered in frames, requiem for the brides
and the grooms and their children. Requiem
for the kids who built the tree fort I set
on fire, requiem for the fathers who
helped them, the big brothers who helped, and requiem
for the sisters who were not invited
to help, or to visit, but wanted to.
Requiem for the picture windows
exploding into the front yards, requiem
for the flower boxes and the rows of
hedges covered in glass, requiem for
the front yards, the bicycles with the melted
seats smoldering on the front lawns, the scorched
playpens stripped of their mesh, the hedges stripped
of their leaves. Requiem for my neighbors

running from their homes in flames, requiem
for the family members who watched their
family members burn. Requiem for
the families who watched their houses burn,
and requiem for the teenagers who
laughed at those burning houses, those burning
neighbors. Requiem for the neighbors
who did not like me, and requiem for
the neighbors who did. Requiem,
requiem, requiem.

Requiem for the shrubs and the hedges,
requiem for the maples and the vines.
Requiem for the housewives who spent their
afternoons drinking Schmidts from wide-mouth
bottles and requiem for their kids who
spent their afternoons hiding from them.
Requiem for the garages, and the cars
in the garages, and the lawn mowers
that caught fire and exploded, and the gasoline
cans that exploded, and the yard tools that
incinerated against the garage
walls, and the insulation that caught fire
and sent spumes of noxious fumes into
the atmosphere above the developments.
Requiem for the developments.

Requiem for Shoridge Hills and Shoreham
Village. Requiem for Shoreham Estates
and Blackfoot Trail alongside the sod farms.
Requiem for the sod farms, and for

the black families that worked them, whose kids went
to school with the white kids and were
invisible. Requiem for the invisible.
Requiem for John Street and the model
homes vandalized a dozen times before
occupancy, and fire. Requiem for
the chapel with the missing statue of
the Virgin, and requiem for the brothers
who stole the statue, and covered its head
with straw and a Nazi helmet, cradled
a toy machine gun in its arms. Requiem
for the brother who went to Vietnam.
Requiem for the brother who went to jail.
Requiem for the brother who robbed a
bank in Oakland, and requiem for his
sister who died of AIDS. Requiem for
the family of fourteen whose home overlooked
the Sound, whose children became nuns and priests
and car thieves. Requiem for the childless
couple who chased us from the empty lot
alongside their quiet Cape Cod into
the woods they thought they owned. Requiem for
the photo products factory, and its
open pit for waste in the woods alongside
the tree fort I set on fire. Requiem
for its waste, that caught on fire but did not
burn. Requiem for the smoke off that waste,
the lungs it seared, and the blood those lungs coughed.
Requiem for the radio tower
that transmitted news of the fire to the
surrounding towns. Requiem for the towns.

Requiem for Calverton and Wading
River. Requiem for Rocky Point and
Miller Place. Requiem for Suffolk
County. Requiem for the potato
fields and the 7-Elevens, requiem
for the backstops and parking lots and dumpsters.
Requiem for the hitchhikers and for
the cars that did not stop. Requiem
for the patrol cars that did, and requiem
for the patrolmen. Requiem for
the legless veterans who drove souped-up
Chevys with hand controls and pedal
extensions while smoking joints and drinking
beer and listening to Grand Funk Railroad
on eight-track tape decks. Requiem for
the GI bill that sent those veterans
back to school where they flipped off the flag or
burned the flag and patrolled the streets around
high schools when classes let out. Requiem
for the flags that burned on poles outside
the high schools and junior high schools. Requiem
for the schools, for the texts that went up in
flames in the schools, requiem for
the janitors and teachers and principals.
Requiem for the childhoods they wrecked,
the minds they destroyed. And requiem for
their childhoods, their minds. Requiem for
it all. Requiem, requiem, requiem.

II

spring leaf
on the reef bottom
drifting this way, that

MANPOWER

The Manpower temp agency sends me
to a railroad crew outside Columbia,
South Carolina. Red dirt, cold pines,
pickup trucks covered in mud, and thermoses
that smoke when you spin off the sealed tops.
Soup, coffee, chicken in tin foil out of
metal lunch pails. I'm the only white guy—
a kid, and they laugh at me like I'm
Leave-It-to-fucking-Beaver. Give me
cigarettes, invite me to dinner, half
the time cracking jokes I can't understand.
Some because they're about sex—I'm no virgin,
but shoving plugs into a wall socket
doesn't make you an electrician.
Foreman named Elrod, a thickset dude
like some villain off TV wrestling,
carries railroad ties under each arm. Gets
impatient watching how the rest of us
two-man singles. We lay tracks, bust tracks up.
A lot of steel, a lot of wood soaked
in creosote, the kind of grease in coveralls
you can't scrub out with a wire brush. And these
big-ass spikes an inch thick and six inches long.
Elrod sinks them with one swing of the sledge,
every time, clear down to the clang of the metal.
My best is seven, not counting all the misses.
White boss pulls up. Elrod shouts, "Police up your
shit, boys." On go the orange hardhats.

Yes boss, no boss, then up your ofay white
ass boss soon as he walks away. Next hour,
no jokes, no smokes, no roaches pressed between
fingers out by the blue Port-o-Sans. Don't
worry, kid, it ain't you, they assure me.
But it is me. It's me everywhere I go.

BLOOD BANK
after Dorianne Laux

When I was sixteen years old and did not
need sleep to feel rested, or a job for
money, I joined the veterans outside
the Camp Street Blood Bank at seven a.m.
where they smoked cigarettes peeled off
the cobblestones and drank MD 20/20
from pint bottles. They wiped their mouths on
the greasy sleeves of fringed jackets or jungle
cammies, looking for a piece of cardboard
or some old magazine to slap on the spit
and piss and vomit laminating
the sidewalks they slept on. I did not feel
soiled by the filth on their fingernails,
the grease in their hair, or the gravel in their
throats. I was enthralled by the lies they told
about where they'd been, what they'd seen, how
many they'd killed, and the way they told those
lies, as if they believed them. As if I
believed them, too.
                                                      Inside the clinic
we reclined on hard gurneys, flies lining
the rims of Dixie cups filled with urine.
"Shame, Shame, Shame" on the radio,
unlicensed nurses in tight white uniforms
dancing the Bump between rows of our
worn-out soles. They pushed thick cold cannulas
in our arms and our bloods drained into

plastic tubing. Arterial blood, slow
and thin. Blood over the legal limit, blood
so dirty it had fleas. Blood of our fathers
who'd disowned us, blood of our mothers
whose faces we'd failed to erase. At night,
I'd be back on Bourbon Street, a pint low,
a dollar flush, Buster's beans and rice glued
to my ribs. Blue notes from clarinets
and guitars joining the termites spinning
in the halos of street lamps, go-cups crowning
the trash cans and dribbling into the gutter
with the butts and the oysters and the sweat
off the shower-capped, jheri-curled tap
dancer from Desire Project scraping spoons
across the slats of a metal scratchboard.
Hawkers barking at the swarms of tourists
gawking at strippers in storefront displays,
and the runaway girls at the topless
shoeshine spit-shining white loafers
on the feet of insurance agents from
Mutual of Omaha. The veterans,
my blood brothers, they'd lurk in the shadows
and scan the sidewalks for half-smoked butts,
and I'd help them put together the lies
they'd tell to strangers tonight, and repeat
to me in the morning, forgetting half
of those lies were mine, and I'd forget, too.

FRENCH QUARTER, 1974

On Bourbon Street, a man who doesn't
drink hawking his poems to a crowd

that doesn't read on a Friday night when
the legs of a stripper poke through

a second story window every seven
seconds and the Runaway Kid nibbles

a 99¢ sukiyaki from a stick
near a cart selling Lucky Dogs.

"Get away from me, kid, you bother me,"
says the Lucky Dog salesman, as he krauts

up another dog for the overweight
tourist the Kid panhandles for change.

The Runaway Kid's been missing
for six weeks, his employers the local blood

banks, his arms a pin-cushion of missed hits
and half-purple bruises. "If you don't buy,"

the poet drones, "I can't sell." The Kid
wipes his fingers on napkins he nicks

from Lucky Dogs, he pockets the change
he cadged off the tourist, and he buys

a poem. "A love poem," he tells the poet,
who says in the end they're all love poems,

and the Kid stands below the strippers' legs
for hours, reciting, until the bouncers

shrug, and the strippers smile, and the tourists
take his picture, almost as if he's home.

THURSDAY NIGHTS, NEW ORLEANS
after Nick Flynn

Looped, wrecked, knackered, bent,
shit-faced, blotto, twisted
out of my fucking tree,
gourd, skull, off my coconut,
off my stool, onto the floor,
into the sawdust, the spit,

the land of the smoking butt,
the fallen change, the crumpled fin
or sawbuck. Up for a taste,
a nip, a wee dram, a finger, a floater,
one for the road. Who the fuck
are you? Looking at, I mean.

Who the fuck are you looking at?
Who's your friend? She got a sister?
Her sister read Proust? Anaïs Nin?
Fried, toasted, damaged, reduced.
Feeling no pain. Cross-eyed, blind,
seeing double, barely functional,

batteries low, unable to launch,
poor signal, zero connectivity,
running on fumes, running on empty,
unable to run, unable to stand,
walk a crooked mile, walk a straight line.
Lines can be straight, and streets,

but the human liver? *I left my liver
on* St. Peter Street. Cirrhotic,
vestigial, fatty, swollen,
over-worked, over-used, over and out.
Dry, thirsty, jonesing, half-shot,
half-crocked, half-a-load, one quart low.

I'll have another—a bump, a shooter,
beer back, a draft, a pint, a pitcher.
Fill 'er up, I'm not driving. Totaled,
around the bend, over the legal limit,
over the cliff, hitting the bricks
before the bricks hit me. The quality

goes in before the piss goes down.
What's yours? What he's having.
What *she's* having. Why not? Don't mind
if I do. Top it up. Do it again.
Don't be bashful. Make mine a double.
Cheers, mate. A go-cup, a six-pack to go.

Gets you where want to go. When you're
having more than one. The whole nine yards.
Forty miles of bad road. Ninety miles
an hour down a dead-end street. Three sheets
to the wind. Wasted and wounded.
Down twice, up once. I said

who the fuck're you looka . . .

YOUR FATHER ISN'T FEELING WELL

Your father isn't feeling well.
He doesn't mean the things he says.
When he's lucid he asks for you.
The hemlocks you planted are dead.

He doesn't mean the things he says.
I know—it's not your problem.
The hemlocks you planted are dead.
You shouldn't hold it against him.

I know it's not your problem,
his nightmares wake him screaming.
You shouldn't hold it against him,
Grandma beat him with a shoe-tree.

His nightmares wake him screaming—
you don't forget neglect, abuse.
Grandma beat him with a shoe-tree.
The way you're living scares him.

You don't forget neglect, abuse,
all passed out on your neighbors' stoops.
The way you're living scares him.
Remember where you come from.

All passed out on your neighbors' stoops,
drunk, you always ask for him.
Remember where you come from.
Your father isn't feeling well.

BARMAID OF THE DAWN
for Colleen Coelho

She's heard it all before, this barmaid
of the dawn, so it's just as well you can't
say it, or anything, your tongue

like an empty wallet in the back pocket
of your face. The way she flips through magazines
in the glow of the silent jukebox,

her tennis shoes white as loose leaf and her hair
shining like ink spilled across a page.
It could form letters, this ink, make words, sentences,

a story, but how would that story begin?
Once upon a time, probably—same as yours.
Against the zinc, someone's old lady

with two black eyes snores into an ashtray.
The TV's on mute above bottles on the top shelf.
Black tears pour from the eyes of Tammy Faye Bakker.

If you're not from here, and you're not, things
can start to look like some sad joke, but you've
been saying that about pretty much every place

you've ever seen from a barstool at four a.m.
The star of *Then Came Bronson* enters, tells
the barmaid who he is. She folds the magazine,

says, "Then came who?" And he leaves.

STOOL SAMPLES: VIEUX CARRÉ AUSTRALIA

for Jessen Nichols

Without warning, the off-duty cop bolts
off his barstool pistol drawn, wheels and
unloads seven shots into the life-sized
cutout of Crocodile Dundee that once

stood at the bar's entrance. "I fuckin' hate
Australia," he explains, and shoulder-holsters
his weapon. Not a sound—from the bar,
the pool table, even the jukebox falls

silent. Till: "Drinks for everyone," he tells
the horse-faced bargirl, and as everyone
steps softly to the bar, the off-duty

cop back pedals out a side door. For hours
the bargirl keeps serving. The cop does not
return. The talk steers clear of Australia.

STOOL SAMPLES: VIEUX CARRÉ DERRINGER

That afternoon, Paul breaks his arm in a
Magazine Street car crash involving him
and a stolen Dodge that hits and continues
to run from the NOPD patrol cars
in chase. *Story of my fucking life*,
he thinks, looking at his limp appendage.

That night, he's back behind the bar, limping
when it's his arm broke, not his leg. "It's all
connected," Paul explains to the impatient
drunk who'd complained. "Maybe if you'd gone to
the hospital," the drunk says, "had it set."
Paul pulls a derringer from his makeshift

sling, point blanks it at the drunk's head. "How 'bout
I send you," he growls. The drunk says, "With that?"

STOOL SAMPLES: VIEUX CARRÉ MIRACLE ON DECATUR STREET

For fifteen minutes in late December
every barstool on Decatur Street empties
and every drunken regular stumbles
outside with arms wide open in the snow
falling in chunks through the wet black night.
There are cheers, cries, and one broken ankle.

Back inside, any money left scattered
on the bars is gone. Was it worth it, some
ask. Others say you don't put a price on
miracles. "Weather ain't a miracle,"
a newcomer says, and he becomes a
suspect. So does the bargirl coming out

of the ladies' room holding a toothbrush.
"Don't look at me," she says, and they don't.

STOOL SAMPLES: VIEUX CARRÉ
THE DREAMS

For his third drink of the day Paul switches to
vodka. It gives a cleaner pain next morning,
a sweeter blood in his puke. The vodka
dreams, though, they'd become a problem—

like his daughter in the Marines, for Christ's
sake, just like her old man. Last time he
spoke to her was the last time, whenever
that was. And his son—well, he was okay

up till the accident. Mezcal drowns those
ghosts but it sizzles his ulcers like clams
in a wok. "Someone play a god damn sad

song," he shouts at the tables where no
one sits. The bargirl slides him a quarter.
"Mezcal?" she asks, as if that's gonna help.

STOOL SAMPLES: VIEUX CARRÉ HERE YOU COME AGAIN

The bet is he'll drink every beer backwards
alphabetically. His friend isn't
biting. "They serve Dixie and Bud," the friend
says. "You in or not?" he asks. "Not. Give me

a real bet, I'll bet," the friend says. On
Letterman Dolly Parton sings "Here You
Come Again." He says, "From the halls of big
bazoomas." "To the shores of Triple-E,"

the friend says. "Not bad," they agree, clicking
bottles. Couple hours later he says,
"What if I drink them forwards?" The friend says

there's no difference. "There's a difference," he says,
and drops it. The friend works an eight-to-five.
He leaves before six to get some sleep.

STOOL SAMPLES: VIEUX CARRÉ
THEY ALL SAW IT

The Indian drank alone, depths of black
sorrow in his eyes. Personal sorrow,
tribal sorrow, who knew? He had it all,
this Indian, and he drowned it alone.

"Yo chief," some drunk said, "what you got, trouble
back in the wigwam?" A second said,
"Another brave kicking in your teepee?"
A third said, "How!" The barman sensed trouble.

"Don't mind them, Tonto," he said, sliding a
shot the Indian's way. "Firewater,
on the Great White Father." That's when it happened.

The Indian stood up, eyeballed
each drunk, turned and walked out the door.
The man refused a drink. They all saw it.

STOOL SAMPLES: VIEUX CARRÉ
THE WORD ON AUGIE

The word on Augie was that he'd raped some
white chick on the pool table past closing
time up at Heartbreak. "There is no closing
time at Heartbreak," was what he'd say but he

never denied raping the white chick.
She was on spring break from a New England
college, she came on strong, she went down hard,
and Augie, he kind of closed the deal. "Chick

said she majored in Econ," he'd say, "and
I just showed her how a man do bidness."
When his body was found on Wisner
out by the golf course, no one connected

events. The rape was six weeks old, no one
knew the victim. Still, you get suspicious.

STOOL SAMPLES: VIEUX CARRÉ BREAKFAST

In Heartbreak a half hour till sun-up
the barman dances with his best friend's wife
to George Michael's "I Want Your Sex,"
a loaded handgun tucked into his

beltless jeans. Opposite the jukebox
the game of 8-Ball in the green felt glare
stops on a sloppy break that sends the cue
ball rolling between the legs of a bride

from Indiana whose husband is
interested, he tells the barman, in some
breakfast. That gets a laugh from the few of
us still hearing in English. The barman

says, "Well, we could all use a little breakfast."
The couple laughs like they heard some kind of joke.

STOOL SAMPLES: VIEUX CARRÉ HORSE COCK

"This horse cock here," Dayshift Don explains
to the boys, tapping his palm with the club,
"you smack a nigger's head with this, it hurts."
"Hurts the nigger?" the boys ask. Don says, "What

are you stupid? Yeah, the nigger." "But it
would hurt a white guy, too?" "I never used
it on a white guy." "But you have used it
on black guys?" "Not yet," Don says, sliding the

horse cock under the register. "Fuck is
this, interview school?" At the bar's other
end, the lifers don't ask questions. They drink,
maybe stare at the wet rings on the bar.

A black guy comes in. The boys say, "Yo Don,
look—a black guy." "Hey," Don says, "black guy this."

STOOL SAMPLES: VIEUX CARRÉ LEBANON

On the news, Lebanon goes up in smoke.
Don switches for the Cards' game. No one lifts
an eye. A soft space maybe a yard from
each man's face, and one woman's, holds their gaze
for hours. What is in that soft space? What do
they see that Don can't? Maybe he could sell

that space for ads, cash out and retire.
Where would he go? Lauderdale maybe, West
Palm, although with his gut he looks like shit
on the beach. Maybe Reno, keep his shirt
on, play some slots. Not Lebanon, that's for
sure. Although it didn't look bad before

the Jews got in there with the bombs. He turns
back to the news, lights a smoke. God damn Jews.

STOOL SAMPLES: VIEUX CARRÉ OLD CHICKEN

Tony the Cuban provides more than just
drinks. He's *lived*, he has a *world view*. He leans
toward the boys to assess their problem.
"*Too old?*" he says, looking down the bar at

the woman who drinks alone. "Old chicken
makes good soup." The boys snicker. Tony shrugs.
Later, after the woman has gone, there
is nothing to live for. Again. "She'll be

back," Tony assures them. She isn't there
the next night, but a fat woman is. "*Fat?*"
Tony says. "Meat is for men, bones are for

the dogs." The boys send her a Chablis. "Up
both your asses," she says. Tony reassures
them. "The unwilling horse gives a good ride."

CONSTRUCTION

Saturdays were half-days, our pockets
full of Friday money. We'd roll over
to the roadhouse on Elysian Fields,
straight-claw hammers hanging from our belts.

The jukebox played "Layla"
and "I See the Want To In Your Eyes."
Pitchers of Dixie, package of smokes,
maybe a Stewart's sandwich from the microwave.

Coeds from UNO bent over
the pool table, denim skirts riding their thighs,
bootheels off the floorboards. I promised
myself I'd chat up one of those cowgirls.

Saturday afternoons I made lots of promises.

A VIEW OF THE RIVER

In those days I lived on the fourth floor
of a French Quarter townhouse. Through
its exposed beams I felt my neighbors'
nightmares. The books they tossed became
my books. In late afternoons I took
my coffee black and unsweetened.
Outside, freighters hung
in the wide bend near Algiers. My friends,

all drunks whose names I barely knew,
were lawyers and waiters and methadone
addicts who encouraged me
to go home. But I was between musics,
my wall of albums gathered dust below
the bricks. At dusk termites spun
in the halos around streetlights,
then came the bats.

BORDELLO: PORT OF SPAIN

In the sitting room where the men make
their selection, the large women in white
underwear smoke blunts the size of Coronas
and drink Guinness from brown bottles.

He was thinking Lena Horne or Dorothy Dandridge
but these girls look like they could carry one
of him under each arm easy. Tonight, this blind
drunken night, his mantra is *stupid, stupid, stupid,*

and he can almost hear himself chanting it when
the petite Asian girl in the gray t-shirt emerges
from behind glass beads and he says, "Her."
Hand in hand, they pass the linebacker-thick guard

in shades who stands behind crossed arms and enter
a doorless room where she asks, "What you like?"
and he tells her everything, everything he admires
about Asians, and it looks like she actually listens.

AT A WINDOW IN X

Because the history of his nation
is tragic, the man stands at the second

story window of a brothel in
another nation and stares into

the distance, a mix of sunshine and rain,
of banana trees and ice caps,

of volcanic ruins and island dogs.
His t-shirt is clammy from exertion.

His dick retreats into its unexcited
pose. He is thinking about his wallet

in the back pocket of his pants, on a chair
alongside the sink, and perilously

close to the hooker with one leg
up on the sink's edge taking a first

wet swipe at the residue of their
transaction. He is thinking that if he

was still a smoker, he would be smoking
now, blowing soft rings into the dirty

window above the lazy street and
allowing the hooker to lift a few

bills from his wallet, although she's already
been paid, and then some, because he feels

guilty, because he feels complicit
with some vast network of injustice,

because he is weak and she is poor, because
the history of her nation is tragic.

He is thinking that she is thinking
that he's testing her, that the instant

she reaches for the pants he'll shout,
and the brute with the huge forearms

and the Chicago Bulls cap will burst
into the room and beat her with

the electric cord that dangles from his belt,
and downstairs he will be given

a Guinness and an apology
and perhaps another girl, perhaps

her sister, who is prettier, and younger,
and more frightened, and more costly because

she is inexperienced, but she will be
experienced by next week because

the history of her nation is tragic.
Later, he'll take his lunch in a café

on Queen Street, where he might take up smoking
again, where he might flirt with the waitress,

where he might forget about his guilt
at the window, until the next window.

OUT WEST WHERE HIS BEST FRIEND SUFFERS DEPRESSION AT HER GRANDMOTHER'S SPREAD

In the morning the grandmother shows him
the rattlesnake twisted around the chicken

wire, knotted up worse than a curtain cord,
back and over and through a dozen holes.

"It gets in," she says, "but it can't wind out—
the head forgets where the tail's been. Sound

familiar?" He's just come from her
granddaughter's bedroom, cotton-mouthed and guilty

as a wet dog slinking off a sofa.
They'd made awkward, hungover love, the bed

frame banging the walls. "She's sick,"
the grandmother continues, "don't you know that?"

And before he says ma'am she says, "She thinks
her daddy raped her. My son." She stamps

a foot on the dry ground, her white socks limp
at her slippers. "Is that what these doctors

tell her?" He avoids the blaze of her eyes,
and she gives up. With a weeder she pokes

the snake. It's too exhausted to rattle.
He says, "I guess I might believe her."

She says, "Oh you might, might you? Isn't that
loyal." She turns for the house, muttering.

"Poking around in all them holes . . . getting
its damn self killed . . ." He finds a stick, tries

to push the snake free, but his help digs grooves
into its flesh and flies drop onto the wounds.

Red ants proceed up the wire, and blackbirds
on the fence posts throw patient shadows.

BROKEN THINGS

I went away and came back the next year.
I found the window still broken. Broken,

still. Everything changes, we know that. We
have changed. But the broken things stay broken.

How broken must we get to reach that kind
of permanence? Permanence exists, no

matter what they insist. Look at it, there,
in the glass that fractures your reflection,

that draws blood from my tongue. It tastes ancient.
It tastes like the beach where we made our vows

and broke them. That beach has changed, it is gone,
but our vows remain forever broken.

MY FATHER HAS A DREAM

He descends a stone staircase.
The stone walls sweat,
the air is heavy.

He's in a prison,
a stone walkway lined with cells.

Outside my cell, he does a double-take.
He says, "What are you doing in jail?"
"You don't know?" I say.

"You're the one who put me here."

He slides out of bed,
not disturbing my mother.
He walks the dogs to the beach.

Across the Sound is Connecticut.
I'm in the other direction.

WEST INDIES HAIKU #1

a white seabed—
the imprint of a ray
no longer sleeping

queen's highway—
a hermit crab tucks
against traffic

two crows
lifting from roadkill—
passing jogger

finches
on the power lines—
empty airstrip

high noon—
the dogs sleeping
beneath a Buick

cactus branch—
a seagull perched
between thorns

rainstorm
at slack tide—
sagging hammock

FOR CHRIS LUNN, WHO BECAME A PARAPLEGIC AT TWENTY, IN AN AUTOMOBILE ACCIDENT NEAR SETAUKET, OCTOBER 1974

That night I was a thousand miles away,
crossing the Gulf Stream from Miami to Morgan's Bluff.

The full moon laid a golden carpet over the lake-flat water.
And the stars!—too many to cram into our cramped galaxy.

Didn't the horizon seem endless?
We radioed ships half the way to Cuba.

By dawn, the foredeck was silver with flying fish,
a few of them still struggling.

MORGAN'S BLUFF

At dawn the gulls laugh again.

Two gray angelfish ascend . . .
. . . kiss the surface . . .
      . . . recede . . .
          the water's surface wrinkles.

Pink light separates the gray sky from the gray sea.
Enormous clouds form like the aftermath
          of great explosions.

How pensive this daybreak,
        a grenade without a pin.

In a needling insect heat the dawn's final breeze fades.

A jeep's lights flash on; it backs out of the commissary.

Pelicans lift from the pylons.
The Cuban whore retreats up the Bluff Road,
        her sandals dangling from a finger.

TONGUE OF THE OCEAN

Before dawn I boil water in a dented pan
set over cans of Sterno. The coffee is poison—
I drink two cups with sugar while preparing
my gear: torch, tanks, sling. I spit in my mask
and back-roll off port into dark water.

Shadows of the nocturnals rush dark gray
over the rubble, my heart thumping in the wetsuit.
Marauding jacks strike at my bubbles, and barracuda
flash silver as new dimes in the chaos before my mask.
Something is out there.

What I kill I gut and clean and sizzle in a pan with onions.
My hands stink of the sea, a funky saltwater conch stink
that forms my pillow at night. Nights light up
like a thousand cruise ships sliding over each other
on pages of blue-black ink.

I read the sky the way we were taught not to read books—
with superstition and wonder and fractured syntax,
without logic, causality, or motivation. I put *e* before *i*
and I tear the night's footnotes into confetti. I fall asleep
dreaming of what I might kill for breakfast,

hungry and satisfied and afraid.

BLUFF ROAD

On a night without stars I walked along
the Bluff Road hoping nothing large would trip
me up. The surf, a minor wrinkle, curled

green with bioluminescence over
the reef, then gently joined the mangrove shoots
in the puddles my sneakers squished into.

My feet were wet. As usual my father
was on my mind, even if I didn't
know it then. Knowing it now doesn't change

the way the path leaned into the mouth of
a dog who bit before barking as if
he knew better than I did what was on

my mind. The ghost with the straw hat lived there
alone, laughing. But it didn't sound like
laughter then. Not much did, not even my own.

LOOP CURRENT
for Tom Miller

At sunrise we piss from the upper deck
onto the flat calm surface of Biscayne Bay.
We are eighteen, the deck is high—our piss
arcs out in glorious loops, splashes with
a bracing violence, its ripples rolling
past the breakwater into the canal
linked to Government Cut where tugs push
cruise ships toward the Gulf Stream, our piss following.
I imagine it churned up in the whitewash
of giant propellers, swirling in a blend
of seas and plasmids as it joins the world's
great currents, hugging the Atlantic
coastline heading north past the flashpoint
of the Civil War, past New England and
Nova Scotia into the vast schools
of bluefin tuna spearing the water
columns. Ice floes threaten shipping in
the North Atlantic. It's lunchtime in
the UK, in Spain they're napping. What drum
beats along the coast of Senegal, what
hurricane amasses? This will be news
in Guyana, news in Jamaica where
from Lucea to Oracabessa
shutters are pulled tight. And traffic
on Route 1 backs up past Matecumbe Key.
By the time we shake off, the coffee cools
in the galley in mugs that taste of bleach,

and local birds vector south in airstreams
miles long beneath the pink and aqua sky.
No news but the weather, no desire
but for longer, and still longer days.

SUNRISE DIVE

News this morning of oil spills on the reef,
where a parrotfish sleeps on a limestone
ledge inside a sac of its own mucus,
its eyes wide open.

Under my torch the mucus glistens
like beads on a veil. The sac undulates
in soft currents,
and the parrotfish wobbles,
imperturbable.

The bad news comes most mornings.
You can read it in the garbage wedged
            into patches of finger coral
a dozen yards out, where the reef shelf drops straight
down a thousand feet.

At the edge
of my torchlight, a bull shark noses the wall. She's there
most mornings, too, when

things on the wall pretend not to be things—
it's an anxious time, a drama on the edge of great violence

most of us will survive.

My torch beam inches gently along the corals.
Antennae recede, spaghetti worms

retract, feather dusters
vanish,

and cleaner shrimp tuck into the fingers of anemones
like women pulling in shutters.

A spotted moray snouts
the hollow of a tube sponge,
then, like a cat, nuzzles the saucer of green felt
on a cup coral.

The schools of wrasse and jacks emerge—
they patrol the edge where sunlight reaches them again.

Once I worked for Big Oil. What have I done?

BLUE SURGE, WITH PROKOFIEV

Not far from the coast of Aruba, no
deeper than ten or twelve meters, you roll
weightless in the surge and figure out
a few things you'll never remember but
will always feel. For a while, you have a friend

you can trust here—a loggerhead turtle
the size of a manhole cover who
allows you to accompany her nowhere
in particular. She tilts, you tilt, she glides,
you glide, until she edges past the outcropping

and drops into opaque blue. There's a feeling
of falling when you watch a friend fall,
but when you check your gauges you're really
not far from where the friend left you, at the edge
of the soft corals bending and swaying,

bending and swaying, white water wrinkling
the surface your bubbles climb toward.
The water column is empty. You breathe
down toward the tops of things—blennies poking
like thoughts from holes in the brain coral,

anemones limp as gloves half off hands.
In your mind's ear, Prokofiev's first
piano concerto, its pushing and pulling,
pushing and pulling, at the body,
the trunk, the heart. Nearby, on a head

of bleached coral, the feathers of a crinoid
wave in the current. Everything benign
is predatory, everything passive
lies in ambush. It's a world you understand.

AMERICAN HOTEL, REVISITED
for David Michael Carter

In this room, the throat of a man I loved was opened by a machete. He was found face down on the floor, glass from a bottle of Bacardi stuck in his gums. This man taught me how to chant, how to meditate, how to isolate my pain in a triangle glowing at the base of my medulla. He taught me that I had a medulla. He taught me how to tie a bowline, how to hitch a skiff, coil a line. He said never go on deck without your nose covered in zinc oxide. He said the cheap sunglasses go overboard, the expensive ones last forever. He taught me how to read a nautical map, how to plot a course, how to pilot a vessel, and how to bring that vessel to dock. He taught me how to contact the high seas operator, Yankee Tango Foxtrot 1476, and to call home often and not to be embarrassed at the inanities my mother shrieked over the intercom while he doubled over with laughter. He taught me how to read the stars, and the water's surface, and the tides, and the currents around blue holes. He taught me how to read the movements of the sharks, how to load a bang stick, and how to hide spear guns from island officials. He taught me how to pull back the bands of a Hawaiian sling, how to circle a school of snappers, how to choose the right one for breakfast, how to gut it and filet it and sizzle it in a pan with butter and lemon and diced onions. He taught me never to follow a chickcharney, and never to take my eye off a shark. He taught me how to string my catch from a line dangling a dozen feet from my body, and how to release that catch when the sharks cut quick sharp angles. He taught me how to dive deep and ascend slowly, and never to pass through the champagne of my bubbles. He taught me how to harness energy, focus effort, eliminate distractions. That vanity is for the vain, the bottle for drunks, the road for drifters. He taught me to question the myth of Jack Kerouac, and alcohol, and rock and roll, and pussy, pussy, pussy. He taught me to respect the sea, and order, and clear decks. He taught me there's one right way, and a thousand other ways that would make me dead. He taught me how death comes from the left with the snap of a dry branch, and that living was worth dying for. He taught me more on a dive than my father did in a lifetime. He taught me how little I listened. How little I listened.

III

heat lightning—
pages scattered
on an empty bed

TEN HAIKU

dragonfly lifts
from the goldfish pond—
no buzz, no ripples

moonless night—
my shadow hidden
in me

circling the crowd
with two drinks in his hands—
his wife missing

lifting her letter's pages
over and over—
the whirring fan

flies hover over
the empty fruit bowl—
his love gone

autumn—
sneakers dry at the end
of a long run

from the treetops
a dead leaf twirls
into my palm

running lakeside
I feel my debts to God—
mallards laughing

early thaw—
the sidewalk crowded
with diners

sidewalk café—
an old friend filling her face
with salad

BALLET

People laugh when I tell them I took
ballet, as if to say, *you?!* As if to say

the son of a high school dropout
U.S. Marine Corps DI unschooled lummox

and general brute of a lumpen thug
could never lift into the air and soar

above an audience. Well, I didn't soar,
I didn't climb into the air, but I fluttered

the wings my teacher told me I had,
and I felt their feathers extend, I saw

the dust motes swirl on the floorboards below
and dance dizzyingly into shafts of light pouring

over the rooftop of Klosty's Hardware before
floating back down to the polyurethane.

ARTS & LEISURE

We held hands through all of *Rocco and His Brothers*.
Now, we're divorced.

When the brutal brother Simone raped Nadia, you covered
your eyes with my hand.

That was touching. Later, when you begged me to beat you,
that was not.

When we split, I sometimes thought, ah, if only I'd beat her,
but then what?

What would we have told my mother, who never liked you,
but who forbade me

ever to raise a fist against a woman. In that respect only,
I've been a good son,

but a bad husband? I don't know—maybe a good husband,
but you wanted bad.

I remember how angry it made you when I said I wouldn't
sleep with your friends—

they weren't pretty. You didn't like me to talk while you read
Arts & Leisure.

Did you finally find your brute? You know, *Rocco and His Brothers* is on DVD.

How are your friends? Are you still reading *Arts & Leisure*? I'm still talking.

OPENING

I am opening a place in your mind,
a place I closed in my own long ago.

I want you to enter and return.
I want you to report what you find there,

wherever there is. I want you to tell
me what I was too afraid to find out

for myself, I want you to make it less
scary. I want you to invite me in

so I might finally know where I've been
sending you all along. What will I do

when I'm there? Will it look exactly
like I told you, as if I'd seen it so

many times before? Will I be able
to keep it open? Return? Report?

SIGHTING

Outside
the Fitness Center
I watched you, old lover, quickly bury

your face
inside a wind-filled scarf.
In these two long years that I've missed you,

how you have aged—
so rapidly,
far beyond whatever troubles

I'd caused your pretty face.
How that delighted me, then left me
vaguely sad.

BELATED APOLOGY

I am sorry, old friend, for laughing that time
the tranny blew you in the vestibule

of a Hell's Kitchen walk-up. I know that
my laughter softened your whiskified dick,

but it was the way she rolled *The New York
Times* under her free arm that made me laugh,

not your dysfunction, which was so sad. I
never meant to prevent you from coming.

TO THE BEST FRIEND OF THE GIRL
IN THE MR. PEANUT COSTUME,
HALLOWEEN, 1986

Thank you for agreeing to come with me
into the men's room of Original
Ray's on 82nd & Columbus
while the pie we ordered with the olives,
extra cheese, and anchovies baked
in the brick oven. And thank you
for opening your blouse when I asked you
and for kissing so passionately, like
you meant it when I lifted your ass on
the dirty sink and hiked the school-girl skirt
over your waist and—Christ, I'm
seeing stars here just recalling the way
your saddle shoe rested against a mop
bucket filled with scummy water reeking
with disinfectant and how the smells
we made together in the sewage funk
swirled into the raunch of the room with
the roaches crawling across misogynist
graffiti and the lock half on a door
we couldn't close. And thank you for saying
thank you when I sunk it in and thank you
for making me feel what I haven't felt
in so many years. You were from, what, Maine?
I loved the way your best friend in
the Mr. Peanut costume waited for us
to emerge, the bubbling hot pizza

cooling below the cigarette she smoked
in a holder, like she was the one just come
from the restroom. The pizza was so good.

OVER SUSHI

Over sushi Jill complains about her recent
Supercut, how they trimmed her bangs so high
above her eyebrows she feels bald as Sinead
O'Connor before the conversion.

I think she looks good. I thought Sinead looked
good, too. You've got to have a face that can
support a skin dome: O'Connor had it.
Jill doesn't, but she's nowhere close to bald

as I am—the retreat of the hairline,
the thinning of the central plain, the scalp
and its excematic discontents exposed.

So I find her complaint pro forma,
a way to get a compliment, even
insensitive. The sushi is okay.

NEIGHBORS AT 9 A.M.

Against the shoulder of my neighbor
I absorb each jiggle of the B, each
wobble, each loss of balance, and I wonder
if there's a street in New York that doesn't

move from under the feet, a street you can
find on a map and it's still there the next
time you look for a pharmacy with a sale
on toilet paper. There are days in this

city—you're probably having one now;
why should you be any different?—days when
you want to say go ahead, pull the god-
damn trigger, get it over with. I'm feeling

that way today, bouncing out of Columbus
Circle with the breath of a janitor
hot on my scalp. What's left to feel anymore
anyway? The feeling's been murdered out

of me, my face hidden in the *Post* and
the night sweat still damp on the waistband
of my skivvies. I've no stomach for much
anymore, not even pretzels, and when

I reach work I hope there's nothing left but
cockroaches crawling through smoke. It's that kind
of laugh I could use this morning screeching
to a stop at the nonsense of West 4th.

ANNIVERSARY

Tonight, I have not drunk alcohol for
nine years, an anniversary of rebirth,
but one I fail to mention at dinner
with Ron, who has not drunk in even more,
except for last year's experiment with
wine, five glasses of it, at a club event
at which he was required to sing, and his
habitual use of marijuana
before, after, and in between meals.
Carver did it, is his argument, why
not me? Plus, it boosts his appetite
and he feels the need to bulk up for
the beach: ninety-eight-pound weaklings don't get
the girls anymore. The bread here is good.
It comes with a tomato-garlic dipping
sauce we use to soften hard wedges. I
have just returned from Provincetown, where,
I complain, the natural, nautical state
of things has been erased by gewgaw
boutiques and tourist families and same-sex
couples wide as double-parked cars shouldering
their way down Commercial Street. Ron's eyes
follow a woman's tank-top tan. He nods.
His Provincetown—Ron's from the Sixties—
was different. His Provincetown featured
Norman Mailer losing fistfights nearly
nightly inside and outside the Anchor Bar.
Where have all the anchors gone, we wonder.

But don't forget, Ron says, the natural
nautical state of things in Ye Olde
P-town included a lot of that same-
sex coupling. To wit, he says: *Moby-Dick*.

Ron tells an interesting story about
a woman he met on the ferry from
Boston to Provincetown. This is back in
the Sixties, he reminds me, when a lot
of cool stuff happened. (An example he
invokes frequently concerns the blowjobs
he got from Carly Simon's sister while
his girlfriend, Carly Simon, was away;
Ron moved in privileged circles—the family
fortune had been squandered down to next to
nil, but the manner and the circle would
not be broken, the Carter Family not-
withstanding, he winks.) But the story,
he says, about this chick on the ferry:
It began on the upper deck. She had
a guitar and she picked some canonical
tunes to which Ron knew the words. Ron had sung
in folk and folk-rock combos. He did a
good Ian Tyson, a better Ewan
MacColl, but his years on smack put the fuck
to his voice-box. Still, in the Sixties the voice
was there, as were the balls, so he took a
seat alongside the guitar chick and began
singing along to the tunes she strummed.
"Four Strong Winds," he sang, and "The Young Birds,"
even "Who Knows Where the Time Goes?" on which

she joined him with a brandy-smooth contralto.
She was blonde and full-breasted and the
mini-skirt she wore had about as much
total material as a magazine
opened up to the middle. Ron thanked God,
or whomever one thanked back then,
for his good fortune. And he made plans,
to which the guitar girl assented.
Dinner first, at some lobster place along
the water, and a chaste kiss on Commercial
Street to delay the inevitable,
which in Ron's plan was scheduled for
the next afternoon after a swim and
some wine and hashish. She missed their appointment,
so Ron called and a man, one of her
several roommates, said try the beach so Ron
strolled along the shore, jaunty and undeterred—
it's the Sixties, mind you, when all plans were
necessarily loose, just as loose as
the connections—and there she was, he said,
not far along the shore, seated in a
circle of men with the guitar on her
lap and she waved Ron over. They were singing,
but now the songs she picked had moved into
pop areas that reflected jukebox
tastes Ron had left behind in 1963.
"Walk Like a Man" was one, he remembered,
and "Johnny Angel." He felt kind of funny,
he barely remembered the words, and though
he knew everyone was stoned, still, he thought,
they all laughed a bit too hard at what wasn't

really all that funny in the first place.
His friend encouraged him to sing so he
sang, but his heart wasn't really in it,
no, his heart was in between those beautifully
sculpted legs of hers that were crossed to support
the guitar and it was then that he noticed
something that made him turn his head and
literally, he stressed, involuntarily,
vomit right there into the sand and the
poison ivy because his beautiful
contralto with the world-class cleavage
and the miles-long legs and the half-decent
guitar technique had a dick that, in repose,
was at least as long as Ron's. Of course
I asked what did you do then? Took her
inside and fucked her, Ron said and shrugged.
It was the Sixties. You had to give
anything a chance. And the tits, he told
me, if you could have seen those, well, he said,
you add up all the parts on a person
and percentage them out, this chick scored at
least in the high eighties, and don't tell me
you haven't fucked around as low as the
sixtieth percentile. And lower, I
admitted, but still, how many points do
you detract for a cock? Our salads arrive—

it is early summer, I am dieting
but then I always am. My salad is
greens with raw veggies, dressing on the side.
Ron's is a pile of shrimp and grilled chicken

and eggs and bits of bacon on top of
a bed of lettuce that he manages
to avoid entirely. Why call it
a salad, I wonder, if it's really
just a platter for other things, but
it's not a thought I pursue too avidly.
Ron's story has me unsettled. Or not
the story, but the fucking part. I'm
okay right up to there, but what did it
mean, in terms of categories I'm speaking,
about Ron's sexuality? Was Ron
gay? If so, what was he doing on all
those Craigslist dates that formed the bulk of his
weeknights, the bulk of his conversation?
Was he gay in the past, but straight now?
To whom, I wondered, was I talking and
how did I need to modulate, if at all?
But more important: to whom was he
talking? Was I some phony fuck who espoused
positions I didn't honestly feel?
Did who or what he fucked now or in the
past matter a damn in the moment,
if at all? Of course I knew it didn't
but my stomach wasn't thrown out of whack
by radishes and arugula, no
matter how unappealing a mess, Ron
said, they made. And it struck me as odd,
and wonderful, how you can get knocked off
your wobble board by a friend you think you
know over a dinner, or a drink, or
a story that starts at the menu and

ends up somewhere south of the border.
We proceed to more anecdotes, jokes,
remarks. References to Monica
Lewinsky. Jabs at Kenneth Starr. The check.
On Broadway, Ron objects to snooping
moralists. Closet moralists, too. He
suggests we answer the call of the wild
and grab some dessert and herbal tea and
I decline claiming work and fatigue, those
two chronic afflictions that New Yorkers
suffer the way fish swim water: without
question. On my walk home I find I'm looking
at people differently. How many dicks
swing under those skirts? And how many
swinging dicks can accommodate
contradictions as wide as Ron's as if
they were just ingredients in a salad?

IV

hates water, loves fish
the cat

HE TEACHES HIS WIFE TOM WAITS

Don't expect Don Ho.
Don't expect Frank Sinatra or Tony Bennett or The Beatles.
Don't expect pretty, unless Pretty's in fishnet stockings suck-
ing a lollipop. Don't expect lollipops.
Don't expect beauty, unless beauty's a rainbow
on a greasy puddle. Don't expect answers, or morals, or affir-
mations. For god's sake, don't expect God.

Waits's guys can pray and implore and supplicate until their
pants wear out at the knee—
but their God is absent, he's drunk, he isn't even watching.
That guy on the sidewalk asleep in a puddle of puke
          —he's the hero.
The girl frozen in the grove—that's redemption.
In Tom Waits, virgins watch the clock unless
they're already dead, and salvation's a cute nurse
at the methadone clinic.

Shit you might expect:
—body piercings and tattoos from the era before body pierc-
ings and tattoos
—hammers and anvils and hacksaws and devils who're your
first cousins
—hookers and losers and Cuban-Chinese in bus stations and
diners and St. Louis
—guys who did the same shit I did only they couldn't stop
—guys you might have married except you had to step over
them

—guys who don't know if they have any children, and wom-
en who'd never tell them

Imagine if I'd never turned my shit around—
that might be me shivering under the bridge in a rainstorm.
Imagine that you had no family—that might be you with the
sawdust on your jacket, the broken heel, and the swollen
         liver.
This isn't peace and love and no possessions,
         this is just no possessions.
And no peace.
And love is on the nickel.

This is a hard day's night's day, and night.
This is America.
This is guys sent off to Iraq and coming home their
         girlfriend's married.
This is that piece of shit Bush with a wetback
         shining his boots.
This is Imelda Marcos dancing with Ronald Reagan while
some Mohawk's passed out in the bathroom
         of a Texaco.
This is me getting banged on student loans from the fucking
Pleistocene while CEOs set up trusts in Vanuatu.
Are you getting the picture?

She says, I think so, but you know what?

He says, what?

She says, How 'bout you just put on the fucking music?

RUIN

In this town (at last) there are no ruins
to visit. The town itself is the ruin—
this is refreshing, this belongs in
a brochure. My wife naps inside while I—
I don't even know what to call it—un-
tangle from the windcarved slabs of antiquity.

I'm tired of visiting cemeteries
alive with learned guides. I'm happier
here, on this balcony, in this little
ruin of a nameless nowhere, observing
the cockeyed alignment of Jupiter
and Venus under a crescent moon.

On other planets everything is
already dead, including the guides.

MOONLIT WALK

You walk out on this failed Sunday
under a January moon so full of sun
it throws shadows on the empty pathway
your footsteps have yet to memorize

and you follow the path away from
the motorbikes whining
in nearby hills to the murmurs
of this slow canal. Wood smoke

lifts from chimneys into the moonlit sky,
past closed shutters and clothes half frozen
on lines. Lifting your head, you fill
your nostrils with your neighbors' fires.

When you were a child at the seaside
dwarfed by the surf foaming at your feet,
how could you fake even one step toward the silent ocean?
Now, along this narrow canal, how firm
the footing for the next, the final steps.

WINTER SUNDAY, FIRENZE

In front of the stone houses, their shutters
drawn and smoke climbing from the chimneys,
the sycamores are bare, leaves loiter
at the tires of the silent cars.

Orchestral music from a radio . . .
a woman's face in a second story window . . .
the shops are closed. No aroma of bread
from the *forno*, no chatter outside the *tabacchi*.

At the corner, visitors follow packages
into a taxi. The taxi turns onto *Viale dei Mille*'s
empty lanes. You proceed to the canal,
always the canal, your hands in your pockets,

a Camus without the *Gauloises*.
At the *Ponte alle Riffe*, a grandson drops bread
to the ducks, his *nonno* smiling. And then
it's just you, you and the purling water.

WAKING

I find myself waking heavily these
mornings, my dreams like the shame of a
hangover. I did something wrong, or
didn't but wanted to. Wanted to

very much. My wife is snoring. In the
kitchen I cut up the materials
for today's shake: mango, papaya,
pineapple. They feel like the materials

of a dream I gave up on. Less than real.
Better. I will blend them into the fuel
of a day that will present me with as

many wrong options as my dreams. One day
I will take one, or two. Maybe then the
dreams will stop. Maybe then I'll wake lightly.

TO SLEEP WELL

you must allow yourself
to forget all the cares and the burdens
and the desires that you believe

constitute yourself
and allow, instead, your true self
to emerge, the self that rides bikes

no hands through traffic; the self
that throws rocks at birds; the self
that shoulders a splintered doorjamb

in an effort not to fall off the porch
drunk. And once that true self emerges,
it will pick the pocket of the self you think

you are, the self that hits
the keystrokes, makes the train,
dismisses the class only after the bell,

and when the self you think you are
reaches for its wallet, it will find
instead a flower, a razor blade, a note

that says: who the fuck are you?
And you will laugh, and cry, and laugh,
and your class will see then who

you really are, stripped
of your identity, and it will laugh
and cry with you because you

are not the self you present to them,
who keeps them at a distance
imposed by an institution that pays

you to remember your cares
and burdens and desires,
you are them, every one of them,

and knowing that, remembering
that, your eyelids grow heavy,
your breath deep.

At least that's what you're thinking,
on a couch away from home, unable
to sleep well.

THE GOLDFISH

In a box pond alongside the *lanai*,
the goldfish make orange angles in green
water. The gardener feeds them each day
at the same hour. When his shadow covers
the pond, the goldfish kiss the surface.

He believes they recognize him. "If you
feed them at a different hour," I ask, "would
they recognize you then?" The gardener
appears bemused. "At a different hour,"
he says, "I'm not the same person."

KING COBRA
for Erich Sysak

The dog's barking woke them—
a cobra had entered the house

and now, reared up, hood flared,
the snake stares down the barking dog,

who snaps and paws and feints.
Roy, from Chicago, freezes.

His machete leans near the door
the cobra guards.

Yu, from Chiang Mai,
comes from the bedroom yawning.

With a straw broom,
she sweeps the snake from the house.

It drops between bamboo slats
onto the dark earth beneath the living

room. *Is good luck*, Yu tells him, and falls
back to sleep in minutes.

Roy can't sleep. He sits with the dog.
He watches the day dawn.

He is close to forty.
In two months he will be a father.

He has so much to learn.

THE KOREANS

In the downpour
a pair of cobras slithers

into the resort
and the restaurant empties

of foreigners.
The boy sets his tray of drinks

on a table and runs for the *itak*
he isn't supposed to keep

in his locker, but does. Not
precisely for this,

but he knew one day it would come in handy.
When he returns

the foreigners' faces press
against the windows. The cobras rear

and flare and face the boy down.
One swing

and he slices their heads off.
An older waiter stands on the severed heads

until the jaws stop contracting.
Housekeeping wipes up the blood

with bath towels.
The boy resumes passing out

drinks like nothing
has happened, but he'll never

forget this night.
Even the Koreans tip.

TERMINAL 3 FAREWELL

From behind a row of empty carts,

she watches her daughter inch up the long line.
At her side, her grandson taps at the apps

on an android screen. Her glasses are fogged—

she daubs at her eyes with the hem of her
pink housedress. What kind of a world is this,

she wonders, that separates mothers

from daughters, that turns parents into strangers
to their own children? This world.

Her grandson tugs at the hem of her pink dress.

STATEMENT FROM A BANK
FORECLOSED

I am old enough now
to sublet my apartment
to the children of old friends.
What will they discover here
about their fathers whom
I've betrayed, their mothers,
with whom I've slept?

I picture them pulling
folders from the rickety files,
holding camera negatives
I was too frightened to develop
up to the light. What
would those frames contain? Lips
I deceived, buttocks I separated . . .

would I even recognize
which parts belonged to whom?
Would they? And what
might they imagine? The shaved legs
of an afternoon rubbing
against my cheeks in
a different zeitgeist,

a distant city. Rod Stewart
and the Faces playing
live in the Commons, supporting

a new LP, burly cops lining
the Freedom Trail, tapping
clubs against their palms. A messy
one-bedroom on Hemenway Street,

kitty litter in the pages
of books left open on the floor.
Kafka's *The Castle. The Teachings of Don Juan.*
And the cries
of the early evening
drifting over the buses
on Huntington Avenue.

We never thought
one day we'd be accountable
to people younger
than ourselves. Smoking cigarettes
naked at the dirty windows,
watching the city's first shag haircuts,
the city's first platform shoes,

parade by. We were sleeping
with our professors then,
we were drinking and driving,
we were avoiding jury duty,
showing up hungover
at the interviews that could change
our lives.

I picture them
pulling down the guitar
I never played, its strings slack,
its tuning impossible to peg.
What songs could he have played,
they'll wonder, strumming
absent-mindedly

while flipping through drawers,
a postcard from Paris
beneath socks, a statement
from a bank foreclosed. Paper clips
older than they are
beneath the sofa, on the tiles
beneath the stove.

Much has changed—
the cockroaches are gone.
In the closet a pair of Levis
washed once and never worn again,
the waist size on the patch
like a phone number
before area codes.

It's almost a thrill
to be probed by these aliens,
these Gaga fans
who wonder idly
who we are to tell them
when the rent is due
and how.

NIGHT DIVE

Once on a moonless night
    I lost my companions.
        Their beams were bright
            but I'd edged over

an outcropping into
    darkness and touched down softly
        on a rubble ledge
            where the wall pulsed

with half-hidden forms, eyes
    on the ends of stalks,
        spiny feelers testing the current,
          feather dusters

vanishing
    in a blink,
        spaghetti worms retracting.
          So sadly familiar—

things I desire withdrawing,
    their forms
        disappearing
          the instant

I extend a hand.
    The reef folding into itself
        like a fist. Then,
          from the stacks of plate coral,

the arm of an octopus slid,
        and another, two more,
                reaching
                        for my fingertips,

my palm. The soft sack
        of the octopus followed,
                inching nearer,
                        her tentacles

assessing
        the flesh of my wrist,
                my arm. My heart
                        pounded. Turquoise pink

explosions rushed across
        the octopus's form. At my armpit,
                she tucked in,
                        sliding her arms

around my neck
        and shoulder, her skin
                becoming
                        the blue and yellow

of my dive skin.
        She stayed with me
                such a short time,
                        her eyes,

those narrow slits,
>   heavy with trust,
>   and my breath
>   so calm, so easy.

Above,
>   my companions
>   banged on their tanks,
>   summoning me to ascend.

How we worry when one slides over
>   a ledge. How urgently
>   we admonish the lost ones
>   to turn back.

IN THE EEL GRASS

Slack tide,
        no current for ten minutes.
The eel grass stiff as soldiers at attention.

At the tip of one stalk, a star anemone, cellophane clear,
an ornament in the currentless shallows—
        nothing to reach for, nothing
                to grasp.

Where do I fit in this stillness—
        gray cloud on a green bottom . . .

Before you bear witness, Charles Wright says,
make sure you have something worth witnessing.

Once I witnessed a young hammerhead nosing around
        this bed. I hugged the bottom, clawed into it,
and once, twice, three times the cool cloud of the hammer
        passed over.

Today I watch a shovel shrimp push tiny debris
        from its tiny nest
        again and again
            like a meditation.

It's low voltage, no danger, no thrill—
        I watch till I'm damn near out of air.

MY BACK PAGES

Bye Bye Birdie, A Hard Day's Night
"Like a Rolling Stone"
The Electric Kool-Aid Acid Test
"Howl" and *On the Road*

Tropic of Cancer, Lenny Bruce
The Rolling Stones' *Let It Bleed*
The Autobiography of Malcolm X
Bury My Heart at Wounded Knee

Taxi Driver, The 400 Blows
Sinatra's *She Shot Me Down*
Ulysses, Proust, *Les fleurs du mal*
Where I'm Calling From

Bud Malt Liquor, Apple wine
Lysergic acid, auld lang syne

ONE DAY ON THE WAY TO THE GYM

on Ovington Avenue, on a sunny
Sunday afternoon in late summer
when the air was cool and leaves

that had fallen early crunched
beneath my feet, I heard a young woman
shouting at her father, who bent over

a cane, a canvas field cap covering
his head and the tops of his ears.
He proceeded down the uneven sidewalk

with great caution, watching each placement
of the cane, each placement of the feet,
rarely looking up at his surroundings,

which were mundane. Parked cars, SUVs
mostly, a late model red Camaro
with out-of-state plates, a pair

of Middle Eastern boys on a balcony
giggling alongside a grill from which smoke
climbed, no traffic, and hardly any sound

at all besides the giggling boys and
the faint roar of a commercial airliner
rushing across the sky, a roar so faint

New Yorkers mistake it for silence, and
the young woman, of course, the daughter, shouting.
Shouting right at her father, right in his

ear, shaking her fist at him, too, her finger,
pointing out some behavior, some attitude
that she would no longer accept, ever

again. She wore stone-washed jeans, boots
that narrowed to sharp tips, and wide oval
sunglasses that completely concealed her eyes.

At Bay Ridge Place she spun and hustled off
toward 3rd Avenue. The old man, her
father, watched her disappear. We stood there,

the two of us, in a silence almost
total, except for the faint roar of
the next commercial airliner forming

contrails in the sky. Then, he proceeded
down the uneven sidewalk with great caution,
watching each placement of the cane, each

placement of the feet, bent toward home.

ALARM

Somewhere in this apartment an alarm
is ringing, or beeping, or buzzing,
we can't be sure. It's dark—we barely know
the place, can't even find the light switches.

We follow the sound, whatever it is.
"Are you sure it's not your phone?" my wife asks.
I am sure, but I say I'm not sure—
of anything, anymore, and I'm not.

"If we had your phone we could use its light,"
my wife says, "to find the source of the alarm."
"If we had a light," I say, "we could find
my phone." Something falls, crashes, breaks.

Glass, ceramics, a vase. We're barefoot. One
of us is bound to get hurt. We say, let's
try to sleep. And we try. The alarm continues.
Becomes part of our dreams. Our waking lives.

FOGHORNS

Morning fog thick on the bay—

the deep baying of foghorns,
        baritone, tuba, French horn,

calling to each other from their clouds below the bridge.

The music of caution, the music of warning,
the music of fear.

Our kitchen is quiet. No fog, no warnings.

We see each other clearly, navigate
        the dangers like ships' pilots.

It's the way we've learned to enjoy our breakfast.

It's the way we clear the path to lunch.

ACKNOWLEDGMENTS

Poems from *Requiem for the Tree Fort I Set on Fire* have appeared in: *Full of Crow, Orange Room Review, riverbabble, Frigg, New York Quarterly* (forthcoming), *Softblow, Saxifrage Press, Mandala, Dead Mule, Down and Dirty Word, Asia Writes, InterlitQ, Mandala Journal, Tongues of the Ocean, Gyroscope Review, Sea Stories, Extract/s, Pank, BlazeVox, Unshod Quills, Toronto Quarterly, The Smoking Poet, Underground Voices, The New Poet, Lunch Ticket* ("Amuse Bouche"), *The Tule Review, Word Riot,* and *Pioneertown.*

This collection began in Florence, continued in London, stumbled in Manhattan (where things often do), gathered strength in Manila, variety in Shanghai, and reached a conclusion in Brooklyn, where I was born. I want to thank Dorianne Laux, Carol Muske-Dukes, Alison Hawthorne Deming, and Kim Addonizio, who gave me the most important thing a writer can receive: validation. Jessen Nichols, New Orleans research assistant and companion in the sawdust, gave me the title for the *Stool Samples* sequence. I'd like to thank my students whose work has inspired me throughout the years, especially those who participated in NYU's Global Liberal Studies Poetry Club.

Most important, I give thanks to Deedle, whose insight and patience and companionship guided the gathering of these poems from the very beginning.

ABOUT THE AUTHOR

Author photo credit: Saul Jonas

Educated by jukeboxes and delinquents out on Long Island, Tim Tomlinson dropped out of high school on his sixteenth birthday and began a five-year period of aimless but purposeful drifting that continues to inform his fiction and poetry. He is a graduate of Columbia University's School of the Arts, and a co-founder of New York Writers Workshop where he co-authored its popular text, *The Portable MFA in Creative Writing*. Having lived and published work all over the world, including his recent chapbook, *Yolanda: An Oral History in Verse* (Finishing Line Press, December, 2015), Tim currently teaches in New York University's Global Liberal Studies program and resides with his wife in Brooklyn.